P9-DFA-319

MACHU PICCHU

THE LOST CIVILIZATION

BY CHRISTINA LEAF

Are you ready to take it to the extreme?
Torque books thrust you into the action-packed world
of sports, vehicles, mystery, and adventure. These
books may include dirt, smoke, fire, and chilling tales.
WARNING: read at your own risk.

This edition first published in 2018 by Bellwether Media, Inc.

No part of this publication may be reproduced in whole or in part without written
permission of the publisher. For information regarding permission, write to Bellwether
Media, Inc., Attention: Permissions Department, 5357 Penn Avenue South,
Minneapolis, MN 55419.

Library of Congress Cataloging-in-Publication Data

Names: Leaf, Christina, author.
Title: Machu Picchu : The Lost Civilization / by Christina Leaf.
Description: Minneapolis, MN : Bellwether Media, Inc., [2018] | Series:
   Torque: Abandoned Places | Includes bibliographical references and index.
   | Audience: Ages 7-12. | Audience: Grades 3-7.
Identifiers: LCCN 2016058366 (print) | LCCN 2016058756 (ebook) | ISBN
   9781626176966 (hardcover : alk. paper) | ISBN 9781681034263 (ebook)
Subjects: LCSH: Machu Picchu Site (Peru)–Juvenile literature. | Inca
   architecture–Juvenile literature. | Peru–Antiquities–Juvenile
   literature.
Classification: LCC F3429.1.M3 L43 2018 (print) | LCC F3429.1.M3 (ebook) |
   DDC 985/.37–dc23
LC record available at https://lccn.loc.gov/2016058366

Text copyright © 2018 by Bellwether Media, Inc. TORQUE and associated
logos are trademarks and/or registered trademarks of Bellwether Media, Inc.
SCHOLASTIC, CHILDREN'S PRESS, and associated logos are trademarks
and/or registered trademarks of Scholastic Inc.

Editor: Betsy Rathburn   Designer: Brittany McIntosh

Printed in the United States of America, North Mankato, MN

TABLE OF CONTENTS

WANDERING THE RUINS

In the thin mountain air, you struggle to take deep breaths. Around you, the mountains of the Andes lie in shadow. The sun has not yet risen.

Then, a beam of sunlight creeps over an eastern mountain. Golden light shines on the stone walls and **terraces** of Machu Picchu. What a breathtaking view!

Select Visitors

Only 2,500 people can visit the ruins each day. Peru's government set this number to protect the site.

As the sun rises, you wander the **ruins** and marvel at the skill it took to build the city. The stones of the buildings fit together without any **mortar** to hold them. Stairways and terraces look like they grew from the mountain.

During your exploration, you wonder about the mysterious city. Why build so high in the mountains? What was Machu Picchu's purpose?

A HIDDEN WONDER

Machu Picchu is hidden deep in the forests of Peru's Andes Mountains. It lies just 50 miles (80 kilometers) from the city of Cusco.

N
W — E
S

Machu Picchu, Peru

Urubamba River

Old Peak

Machu Picchu means "old peak" in the Quechua language. The mountain peak south of the city shares this name.

Machu Picchu stands about 8,000 feet (2,440 meters) above sea level. Two peaks tower above it. Far below, the Urubamba River curls around the site.

Emperor
Pachacuti

The **Inca Empire** built Machu Picchu long ago.
Emperor Pachacuti led this powerful **civilization**
in the mid-1400s. Around 1450, he ordered the
construction of Machu Picchu. But after less than
100 years, the Incas had left.

The site lay untouched for nearly 400 years. Then, an explorer rediscovered it in 1911. Today, people travel from around the world to experience the forgotten Inca city.

What a Find!

Explorer Hiram Bingham told the world about Machu Picchu in 1911. A local named Melchor Arteaga led him to the site.

Hiram Bingham

THE ROYAL RESIDENCE

No one truly knows the purpose of Machu Picchu. But researchers believe Pachacuti used the city as a retreat. There, he could relax away from the busy Inca capital, Cusco. Sometimes he entertained royal guests.

Pachacuti chose the location carefully. **Sacred** peaks surrounded the site. The river below was also holy.

Why So Mysterious?

The Incas had no written language. This makes Machu Picchu hard to study. Scientists must use other clues to learn about the city.

terraces

The builders were faced with a difficult task. The site sat high on a mountain. On either side were sharp drops to the river below. Floods and other disasters struck often. These could send buildings sliding down the steep slopes.

Fit for a King

Workers planted corn on the terraces. It was considered a royal food.

The Incas built carefully. They created terraces to secure the city in place. Drains crisscrossed the land to carry heavy summer rains away.

Temple of
the Sun

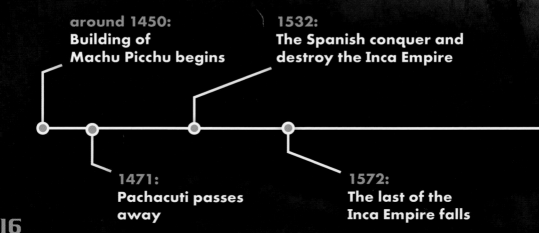

MACHU PICCHU TIMELINE

around 1450:
**Building of
Machu Picchu begins**

1532:
**The Spanish conquer and
destroy the Inca Empire**

1471:
**Pachacuti passes
away**

1572:
**The last of the
Inca Empire falls**

The emperor lived in a palace near Machu Picchu's temples. These temples honored important Inca gods. Smaller houses stood farther away. Servants, farmers, and other workers lived in them.

Many scientists believe people remained in the city after Pachacuti's death. Family mummified the ruler. They kept the body for special occasions. Others think Pachacuti's death was the beginning of the end for Machu Picchu.

1911:
Explorer Hiram Bingham
is led to Machu Picchu

1983:
The ruins become a UNESCO
World Heritage site

STILL A MYSTERY

In 1532, the Spanish arrived in Peru. They brought destruction to Inca cities. Shortly after, the empire was wiped out. Yet, Machu Picchu lay untouched.

Spanish defeat of the Inca

The Spanish probably never reached the mountain site. Over time, the jungle hid the path and the city was forgotten. But why did the Incas leave?

Some researchers believe smallpox spread to the city. The disease killed many Incas. Others think the workers just slowly left. The Inca Empire had fallen There were no more royals to serve

We may never know what happened
to Machu Picchu. But the city in the clouds
stands as a reminder of the mighty
Inca civilization.

GLOSSARY

civilization—an advanced society

emperor—the only ruler of a large territory

Inca Empire—a civilization of native people who lived in modern-day Peru and nearby South American countries before Spanish explorers arrived

mortar—a paste that holds building materials together

mummified—preserved a body with oils and other substances for burial

ruins—the remains of a human-made structure

sacred—holy or deserving respect and honor

sea level—the height of the surface of the sea

smallpox—a sometimes deadly disease that causes a fever and rash

temples—places of worship

terraces—flat ridges on a hillside that help keep the soil in place

TO LEARN MORE

AT THE LIBRARY

Garbe, Suzanne. *Secrets of Machu Picchu: Lost City of the Incas*. North Mankato, Minn.: Capstone Press, 2015.

Lewin, Ted. *Lost City: The Discovery of Machu Picchu*. New York, N.Y.: Philomel Books, 2003.

Morlock, Theresa. *Ancient Inca Geography*. New York, N.Y.: PowerKids Press, 2016.

ON THE WEB

Learning more about Machu Picchu is as easy as 1, 2, 3.

1. Go to www.factsurfer.com.

2. Enter "Machu Picchu" into the search box.

3. Click the "Surf" button and you will see a list of related web sites.

With factsurfer.com, finding more information is just a click away.

INDEX

The images in this book are reproduced through the courtesy of: javarman, front cover; Pavel Svoboda Photography, pp. 4-5; sharptoyou, pp. 6-7; Ilya Paripsa/ Alamy, pp. 8-9; Al Wayztravelin/ Mauritius/ SuperStock, p. 10; Wikipedia, p. 11; Matyas Rehak, pp. 12-13; amadeustx, pp. 14-15; FabioIm, pp. 16-17; North Wind Picture Archives/ Alamy, p. 18; vitmark, p. 19; Patrick J. Endres/ Alamy, pp. 20-21.